To Taste the River

To Taste the River

Poems by Baiba Bičole

Translated from the Latvian by Bitite Vinklers

Plamen
Press
Where Words Ignite

Washington, DC

Plamen Press

9039 Sligo Creek Pkwy, Suite 1114, Silver Spring, Maryland 20901
www. plamenpress.com

Latvian text copyright © 2020 by Baiba Bičole
English translation and introduction copyright © 2020 by Bitite Vinklers
Published by Plamen Press, 2021

Printed in the United States of America

10 9 8 7 6 5 4 3 2 1

PUBLISHER'S CATALOGING-IN-PUBLICATION DATA

Names: Bičole, Baiba, author. | Bitite Vinklers, translator.
Title: To Taste the River / Baiba Bičole; [translated by] Bitite Vinklers.
Description: Silver Spring, MD: Plamen Press, 2021

Identifiers: LCCN 2021911262 | ISBN 978-1-951508-02-9 (paperback)
ISBN 978-1-951508-17-3 (Epub)
ISBN 978-1-951508-19-7 (PDF)

Subjects:
LCSH: Latvian poetry--Translations into English.
Latvian poetry--20th century. | Baltic poetry.

Edited by Rachel Miranda Feingold

Drawings copyright © 2021 by Baiba Bičole
Cover art copyright © 2021 by Serena Faye

The poems have been selected by the translator from the following publications by Baiba Bičole:

Ceļos (Roads) (New York: Grāmatu Draugs Press), 1969 | *Burot* (Bewitching) (New York: Grāmatu Draugs Press), 1976 | *Griežos* (Turning) (New York: Grāmatu Draugs Press), 1981 | *Atgriežos* (Returning) (Riga, Latvia: Liesma Press), 1991 | *Citviet* (Otherwhere) (Riga, Latvia: Mansards Press), 2011 | Poems in *Latvju teksti* (Latvian Texts) (Riga, Latvia), November 5, 2014

Dedicated to my daughter Rita Laima, my son Artis, and their families, and in memory of my eldest son, Arvils (1955-2000). Dedicated to the joys of friendship, the wonder of love, and the exhilarating dance of creativity.

B.B.

For Uldis

B.V.

Contents

III

IV

V

Introduction: *"I Exist Outside of Time"*

Many of Baiba Bičole's poems evoke a sense of time. A poem about the present ends with:

> —*We exist outside of time.*
> *We are thresholds*
> *neither for leaving,*
> *nor returning.*
> *I look nonbeing in the eye,*
> *and I behold*
> *my twin.*

The bleakness here may reflect her experience as a refugee and an exile. Born in Latvia, Bičole left during World War II, and since 1950 has lived in the United States. Though a major Latvian poet since the 1970s, until Latvia's renewed independence in 1991, she was known primarily in the West, as an exile poet, her work banned in Latvia during the Soviet occupation. This is the first collection of her work in English translation.

Baiba Bičole belongs to the postwar generation of Latvian poets living in exile who reached artistic maturity outside their native country and broke with the older exile generation's traditional, nationalistic poetry. Scenes of inner experience, her poems are lyrical and personal, often with intense emotion and startling imagery. Shown through different prisms, like variations on a theme, her subjects include separation, loss, and time; the power of language and song; and love. Central to her vision is nature, both as subject and metaphor. Appearing most frequently are waters (rain, mist, ice, rivers), birds, sun, and sky. Throughout there is a continuing motif of thirst, along with the need for freedom and movement, usually expressed through transformation. We

see her becoming bird, wind, even "a speck of dust from a star."
In "Advice to a Painter," she tells the artist,

> *You marvel and complain*
> *you cannot capture my face*
> *on canvas:*
> > *—paint the iridescence of movement,*
> > *instant of transformation,*
> > *the leap of darkness into light,*
> > *and the inching back.*

Nature in her poetry is distinct in that it is rooted in the world of the traditional Latvian folk songs, the *dainas*, where nature is animistic and personified, and the human and natural worlds are deeply interrelated. But her voice is unique, and her imagery idiosyncratic: the sun is imagined as a dog "tethered / to climbing its mountain"; the earth is "a mouth / that reproaches, that beseeches / the sky"; and bitter cold is experienced as

> *Coldness with tusks, with steaming breath,*
> *and a heart*
> *that demands*
> > *mine.*
> *It searches, finds it,*
> *hides it deep*
> > *within.*

In contrast to the natural world, there is a recurring theme of domesticity. It, too, has a traditional, folkloristic cast to it, for the domesticity is usually not that of today but of an older time, particular to the Latvian countryside, with shawls, peasants' bast shoes, traditional foods.

Yet, in "The One Who Wanted to Get Away," when the person is offered a scene of a bountiful past and a life close to the earth, he chooses instead the pull of the stars, with consequent transformation— and another kind of existing "outside of time," of "nonbeing":

. . . the sharpness
of stars
tickled his shoulders and soles,
tugged each night at his eyelids—
and silent, hidden in thickets,
he became a student of birds:
drawing on cliffs,
with a red sliver of stone, wings,
                                    wings—
and slowly he grew
thin and light as a bird,
as a butterfly, the tiniest moth,
as a speck of dust
from a star.

About the Translation

The first step was selecting the poems and deciding how to organize the book. As I reread Bičole's six collections of poetry (1969 to 2011), related poems from different periods began to cluster in interesting ways, and I felt that organizing the selection thematically, rather than chronologically, would be the more meaningful way to introduce her poetry to the reader, especially since this is the first translation in English.

The three criteria for selecting a poem were the same as for the other Latvian poets I have translated: the excellence of the poem; its translatability into English; and its universality and relevance for the contemporary English-language reader. A later criterion, as the collection took shape, was whether a particular poem belonged and added to the arc of the whole. (To counter the thematic arrangement, in the "Sources of the Poems" I have listed the poems by collection.)

Two characteristics of Bičole's poetry that make it especially hard to translate into English are her complex language and the strong, flowing musicality. Latvian is an inflected language with a very flexible word order, and Bičole makes the utmost use of this. Her sentences are intricately and densely woven; it can be difficult to unravel the syntax to get at the meaning, and even more so to recreate the texture in translation. The musicality of her poems includes a great deal of alliteration and assonance, expanded by wordplay on the same sounds. Although it was rarely possible to use alliteration for the same words in English, I have tried to use it in surrounding words.

A great help throughout was Bičole's excellent English, which allowed us to discuss even minute details of a poem. The work was also made easier and more enjoyable because we have known each other a long time; I felt comfortable asking questions, even naive ones, and she was always ready to answer them and talk about the poems. Indeed, I was amazed at how well she remembered the circumstances and emotions involved in writing a particular poem decades earlier. She gave me great freedom in translating her poetry, and would even suggest cuts or revisions to the original Latvian for a clearer reading and more effective translation.

There were some bright, serendipitous moments along the way. One of the nicest was receiving in March 2020 an e-mail letter from Kevin Morse, whom I did not know, and who wrote: "I am a Canadian composer and university professor currently working on a musical composition for two UK-based performers (soprano and violist) who will be doing a European concert tour this summer. Their theme is 'crossing borders,' and one of their concerts will be at the World Viola d'Amore Congress in Sigulda, Latvia. I recently came across your wonderful translation 'Walking' by Baiba Bičole in the poetry anthology *In Transit: Poems of Travel* (Birmingham, UK: The Emma Press, 2018), and am very interested in undertakig a musical setting for this—and/or other translations of Baiba Bičole's poetry that you think might resonate with the broad theme of moving and travel."

Bičole's poems have been set to music by the Latvian composer Arnolds Šturms, but this is the first time a musical composition was inspired not by the original Lavian but by a translation. Music is an essential part of Bičole's life, and when I told her the news, she exclaimed, "I feel as if I have just been given a huge bouquet of roses!" Because of the coronavirus pandemic all the concerts were canceled; let us hope that someday we will be able to hear this music.

Visual art, too, is central in Baiba Bičole's life; she has drawn since an early age, and for a time attended The Art Students League of New York. Interspersed among the poems are five of her ink drawings, from a notebook of the last few years. Each consists of a single continous, flowing line, the pen not leaving the paper until the drawing is finished. The drawings are made spontaneously, in one sitting, and Bičole experiences the process as a kind of meditation—part emotion, part thought and observation, watching to see what will happen—where she feels completely free. The drawings here are not illustrations to particular poems, but exist independently—visual poems paralleling those in words.

—Bitite Vinklers
New York, 2020

Author's Note

I have always considered poetry in translation as an essential means of becoming acquainted with other cultures, as well as an affirmation of humanism as such. But to experience my own poetry being carried over into another language has proved to be an interesting, enriching event, thanks to Bitite Vinklers's excellent work.

During the course of this book's creation we talked frequently. Suggestions and ideas about textual changes were always done through discussion. Bitite always informed me about what was to be translated or had been translated already, asked for my opinions, expressed curiosity. I was able to trust her completely.

She selected poems from collections published over a range of many years, which led me to step back through time, to reexperience the past, more than once in wonder about the creation of past scenes of emotion. I feel that it was a beneficial way of getting to know myself, or know myself anew.

The poems Bitite has translated breathe, are alive; I read the English texts as independent of the Latvian ones, and I truly enjoy reading them—I experience them as something new.

Parallel to this sense of newness is knowing that no child is born of its mother a second time; every poem has its own and unrepeatable time, its own environment, in which it arrives, and that is the only time.

And what, then, is a translated poem? —It is a key to discovery, it is a key of brotherhood, it is a magician's key. A translated poem has its own, independent existence, it is not an exact copy of the first one, for each language has its own strength, color, form of expression.

—Baiba Bičole
Metuchen, N.J., 2020

To Taste the River

S·G·   16. aprīlis, 2017, Lieldienas

•

—un tad man gribējās nogaršot
upi.
Bet viņa jau bija pasteigusies
iemaukties pazemes ezeros,
pacelties gaisā,
    un es redzēju
    kalstošas siekstas, drūpošus akmeņus,
    oļu un smilšu rotaļu gultnē,
        bet tas jau prasījās citādas
        mutes,

        un tad es sajutu
        sevi sarūkam sīku un mazu,
        sev pieaugam spārnus un
            knābi,
        un ar manu plati atvērto
            rīkli
        vālodze brēca.

"—and then I wanted to taste the river"

—and then I wanted to taste
               the river.
But it had slipped into
underground lakes,
risen in the air,
    and I saw,
    in a playground of pebbles and sand,
    bleached snags, crumbling stones
    that needed a different
             mouth

        and I felt myself becoming
        slight and small,
        growing wings and
            a beak,
        and from my wide-open throat
        the voice of an oriole cried for rain.

Tuksnesis

I

Pār trauku, pār roku, pār lūpām
sausas smiltis trenc vējš.
Vairs slāpēm nezinu vārda,
es vairs neatceros,
kas ir ūdens, avots, aka,
kas tava mute,
es neatceros nekā,
es esmu tuksnesis.

II

Es esmu tuksnesis.
Mirāžu karogus nesot,
ļimstu un ceļos,
ceļos un grimstu,
smiltis mani atrok un apber,
apber un atrok
arvienu sausāku,
izsusējušāku,
smiltis, smiltis
arvien biežāk un biezāk
starp to, kas biju, kas esmu,
kas būšu.

III

Kas būšu? —Tuksnesis.
Būs zilas, zilas debesis,
būs spoža, spoža saule
(cik skaistas dienas!),
būs zelta smilšu
klejotāju cilts.

Desert

I

Across dishes, hands, lips,
the wind is sweeping dry sand.
I no longer know the word for thirst,
I no longer remember
what is water, spring, well,
what your voice is,
I remember nothing;
I am a desert.

II

I am a desert.
Bearing flags of mirages,
I fall and rise,
rise and sink,
sand uncovers me, drifts over me,
more and more parched;
sand, sand
more frequent, heavier
between what I was, am,
what I will be.

III

What I will be? —A desert.
There will be a blue, blue sky,
a brilliant sun
(such beautiful days!),
there will be a nomadic tribe
of golden sand.

•

Zeme ir cirvis,
kas savus bērnus
no sevis
        atcērt.

Zeme ir virpuļojošs šķirsts,
kurā sabirst,
no kura izbirst
            viss.

Zeme ir acs,
kas veselu jūru
            pieraud.

Zeme ir mute,
kas sūdzas, kas lūdzas
            debesīm.

"The earth"

The earth is an ax
that splits off
              its children.

The earth is a spinning coffin
all things fall into,
                    fall out of.

The earth is an eye
that fills an entire sea
                    with tears.

The earth is a mouth
that reproaches, that beseeches
                          the sky.

B.B.   25. nov., 2018

Senmāte

Viņa ir bļoda un karote reizē,
viņā iemērc, no viņas smeļ
vīrs, bērni un saime,
viņa ir gaišs, miltaini kūpošs
                              kartupelis,
balts piens un putraims sīks,
sviesta zeltainā acs
un tumšzaļš, sīvs sīpola laksts,
viņa ir galds, un viņa ir gulta,
no kuras, gadskārtām spraucoties
                              cauri,
izkāpj un pieceļas cilts
un dainu un villaines raksts.

Ancestral Mother

She is the bowl and the spoon at once,
dipped into, sipped from
by husband, children, and household,
she is the light, steaming
                              potato,
white milk and barley groat,
the golden eye of butter
and bitter dark-green scallions;
she is the table, and she is the bed,
from which, pressing through
                              the years,
climbs out and rises a tribe,
and the language of shawls and song.

•

Esmu bungu āda, indiānis.
Noslēpumaini jums pretī dunu,
kad pār mani jūsu pirksti
                                danco;
ļoganām gūžām un šļauganām
                                plaukstām
jūs kustaties manos sirdspukstos,
—ā! jūs jau esat man atdevušies!—
jā, sitiet vēl, drebiniet mani,
mana āda ir bieza, mani kauli
visās kapenēs pretī jums vārtās—
manas zemes zibens krustos
jums pakārties!
—Dūmu mēles jau daino,
vai dzirdat?

"I am the skin of a drum"

I am the skin of a drum, an Indian.
Enigmatically I pulse at you,
as your fingers
                    dance on me;
with loose hips and slack hands,
you move to the beat of my heart—
ah! you've already surrendered to me!
Keep drumming, yes, keep making me quiver,
my skin is thick, my bones
in all the graves are heaving—
on the lightning crosses of my land
may you be hanged!
—The tongues of smoke already sing:
can you hear them?

Atdalītie

Tā sāpe, čūlājoša brūce.
Kā niknā sapnī
ašas sētas
    sastatās
un pārcērt taku,
dobi pāršķeļ,
starp diviem sliekšņiem
sūbru mežus audzē.

Man jaunas zintis raudzēt,
kā stabulēt, kā zīlē vērsties,
kā dziesmu, tālu staigātāju,
dzemdināt, bez maldīšanās
tavos ciemos vest.

Separated

The pain, the festering wound.
As in a fierce dream
where a fence
             springs up
to sever a path,
divide a garden,
where between two thresholds
rises an impassable forest.

> —The need to learn anew
> how to turn into a songbird, give birth
> to song that will journey far,
> not losing the way.

•

I
—šodien
rakstu caur tuksneša
            smiltīm,
šņirkst rakstīklis,
apvārsni bakstot,
            zemi,
ūdeni meklējot.

II
—šodien
meklēju diegu
    salāpīt plīsumu,
    savilkt kopā
        puses
        atšķirtās
        brīdī,
kad likās—
gavilēšu,
kad sapratu—
raustīšos raudās.

"today"

I

today
I am writing through desert
                              sand;
my pen scrapes,
poking at the horizon,
                    the earth,
searching for water.

II

today
I am searching for thread,
        to mend the tear,
        stitch together
                    the separated
                    halves,
        at a moment when it seemed
        that I would rejoice—
        when I understood
        I would be weeping.

●

Vakars salocīts, nolikts
pagātnes pūrā.

—Nebūs ne spuldzes, ne sveces,
ne skala, ne krama neviena,
kuŗu gaismā izvētīt putekļus,
salāpīt irušas vietas,
ievērt dzīparu košu—

vai tādēļ tik tumša nakts?

"The evening has been folded"

The evening has been folded, laid away
in the dowry chest of the past.

> There won't be lamp, candle,
> torch, or brand
> in whose light to shake out the dust,
> mend unraveled places,
> interweave colorful yarn—

> Is that why the night is so dark?

(No Sapņu grāmatas)

—upe. Lēna lēzena laiva
tuvu gar krastu slīd,
iekožas smiltīs, stājas.
Izkāpj sievietes, divas,
viena kā gaišzaļganā pākstī tinusies,
zilganā otra, tīras un dzidras
krāsas. Viņas ir māsas.
      Aizzūd viena no viņām,
      ašu un drošu ņēmusi taku,
      atpaliek otra, aizmirsusi,
      kā sauc pilsētu,
      uz kuŗu tai ejams,
      kā ielu, kā izskatās
      nams, viņa atceras māsu,
      krāsas tīras un dzidras.
            Šķiršanās duļķainais krasts.

(from a dream diary)

A river. A slow, shallow boat
glides along the shore,
bites into the sand, stops.
Two women climb out, one in light green,
as if robed in a pea-pod shell,
the other in blues, the colors clean
and clear. They are sisters.
     One disappears,
     quick and sure of the way;
     the other remains, having forgotten
     the name of the city
     she was traveling to,
     the street, the house; but she remembers
     her sister, the colors clean and clear.
               —Separation's clouded shore.

Pie gleznas

Šo krāsu nesaderīgās māsas,
vienā ielogā iespiestas,
sakostiem zobiem plēšas un
                              cīnās—
to roku, kas dzemdināja
un tagad atpūšas mierīga,
viņas gribētu izplūkt
kā aplamu sakni,

bet viņas ir kā zivis
zem ledus vāka,
viņas kustas un neaizkustas,
viņas raustās un nenoraujas,
viņas brēc, un viņu valoda
ir caurspīdīgi burbuļi
caurspīdīgā ūdenī.

Before a Painting

These colors, these incompatible sisters
pressed together in a single frame,
their teeth clenched, they fight and
                              struggle—
the hand that gave birth to them
and now calmly rests,
they would destroy
like a weed,

but they are like fish
beneath a lid of ice:
they move, and cannot move away,
they jerk, and cannot jerk apart,
they scream, and their language is
transparent bubbles
in transparent water.

•

Saules piliens, zeltains taurenis
iekrīt man plaukstā,
un no viņa kustībām ašām un vārām
es iesāku drebēt,
    —tik tuvu tur kustas
    bailes no nāves,
    no gūstekņa nāves,
    ka manas iztrūcinātās saujas
    kā lūgšanā kaislā,
    kur mīlestība ar bailēm skaujas,
    sakļaujas cieši.

            —Pēkšņi pār mani šūpojas āmen,
                —atvērtā lūgšanas sprostā
                    aptumsums dus.

"A drop of sun"

A drop of sun, a golden butterfly,
falls into my hand
and from its quick, frail movements
I begin to tremble;
     —so near me
     a fear of death,
     the death of a captive,
     that my startled hands
     close,
     as in a fervent prayer
     where love and death embrace.

          Above me sways a sudden *Amen:*
            in the prayer's trap,
              when opened,
                lies eclipse.

Kāda izvadīšana

Dievnama zvans gaisu loba,
mizo un plēš,
un kaili bērinieki
uz izbaiļu trīsām
sēdekļos sagumst—

    maija ziediem apvijies,
    nomirējs ienāk,
    puķu acis,
    puķu sirds,
    ik pirksta galā puķe zied,

        bet dzīvie
        saldami salst,
        un ticības, cerības, mīlestības
        lūdz drānas.

At a Funeral

The church bells pierce,
splinter the air,
and the mourners, naked,
trembling in fear,
shrink back in their seats—

> Wreathed in the flowers of May,
> the one who has died enters:
> a flower heart,
> flower eyes,
> a blossom at each fingertip,

> > but the living
> > grow colder and colder,
> > and plead for garments
> > of faith, hope, and love.

Raudot

No sienām, no grīdas
izmīdītajām spraugām
izaug mitras puķes
sapluinītām malām,
klusām pār vaigu bīdās—
maigas pelēkas sievas
ar pāri līstošiem nēšiem.

Weeping

Out of walls, out of cracks between
worn floorboards,
emerge moist flowers
with ragged edges:
quietly, they move across the cheek,
like gentle, gray women bearing yokes
with pails spilling over.

•

—Tā, it kā šai dienai nebūtu beigu,
nebūtu skaitāmas stundas,
tā, it kā ar milža mēru mērījams
                              laiks—
     kā citādi vienā dienā var
          sāpēt tik daudz,
        mēģināt aizmirst tik daudz,
     atcerēties tik daudz,
          tīrīt un tīrīt sliekšņus, durvis
                         un logus,
        lai saredzētu īsteno sevi,
        saredzētu patiesos citus.

"As if this day were unending"

As if this day were unending,
the hours uncountable,
as if to measure time, a giant ruler were needed—
  how else in one day
  can you feel so much sorrow,
  try to forget,
  try to remember so much,
    scrub and scrub doorsills, doors,
        windows,
    to see your true self,
    to see the real others.

•

Es pagriežos, nē, ne
savam otram vaigam
saņemt pļauku,
    es pagriežos,
    lai saskatītu to, lai
    ieskatītos acīs tam,
    kas cirta pirmo reizi.
      —Visapkārt migla,
          migla,
             migla.

"I turn"

I turn, no, not
to turn the other cheek,
    I turn
    to see the one,
    to look into the eyes
    of the one who struck me
    the first time.
        —All around me mist,
                mist,
                  mist.

(aplenkumā)

—paveras logi, aizdarās ciet,
atlec durvis, uz mirkli
iedejo vējš, izdejo
atpakaļ
ārā, bet stenderes, stenderes
                    atkal
          un eņģes
          stiprinieces, un
          augsti siekšņi, un
          slēdzenes, slēdzenes,
          bruņusievas.

(siege)

—a window opens and shuts;
doors swing open, for a moment wind
dances in, dances
back
out, and again doorposts, doorposts,
    and hinges unyielding
    as warriors,
    and high doorsills,
    and locks, locks,
    like women
    in armor.

•

Biezajiem mūriem cauri spraucoties,
skaņa arvienu tievāka izdilst,
līdz pārlūst pavisam,
un manas lūpas pielīp pie sienas
kā sludinājums
sen pagājušam notikumam.

"through the heavy stone wall"

Squeezing through the heavy stone wall,
sound grows thinner and thinner,
until it breaks in two,
and my lips press against the wall
like the proclamation
of a long-ago event.

(nerunātāji)

I

Mēmumā mist—neatģist, ka mūris paceļas priekšā,
riekšavām savāktie graudi birst ārā,
žāvājas apcirkņi bāri,
un rokas novārgušas
par velti mokās
ap slēdzeni
salūzušo.

II

Bez vārdiem—zārdi jau gadiem bez siena
stāv pelēki, kārni,
tur vējš izsukā matus,
tur sniegputenis
sašķiebj savus ratus,
garām traukdamies.
Stāv kauli bez miesas,
—cik ilgi vēl tā?—
jau zeme apkārt atmatā.
　　Kad nāks, kad sāks
　　tā vētra brēkt,
　　kas zemē trieks,
　　kas saspers, sašķaidīs
　　mūs,
　　kas tik briesmīgi bijāmies
　　īsteno vārdu?

(the mute ones)

I

To live mute—to not comprehend the rising wall,
not see the grain, gathered handful by handful, spilling,
the granary's yawning emptiness,
the frail hands
struggling in vain
with a lock
that is broken.

II

No words ever spoken, for years the hayricks
stand bare, gray, as if emaciated—
there the wind brushes its hair,
a blizzard becomes entangled.
Bones stand fleshless,
the land lies fallow
—for how much longer?—
>   When will the storm come,
>   begin to howl,
>   that will throw us
>   to the ground,
>   strike and shatter
>   us,
>   who have been so terrified
>   to speak the true word?

●

—kad joņo cauri
sper spārda kož
uzkrīt virsū
smagi
tik smagi
zirgi
vētra
nemiers
un vētra
—kā noturies pretī?
ar miera plaši izvērsto
zelta auzu lauku?
—vai: otru nemieru
otru brāzmainu
dārdētāju pulku
pretī
un pret?
—kā? —tā, lai paliktu
zaļa zāle mīksta tumša nakts
ugunskurs pieguļnieks
jājējs mājās pārnācējs
—un mājas
lai paliktu mājas
kur pārnākt mājās

"—when heavy horses"

—when heavy
    such heavy
        horses
            storms
                unrest
                    gallop through
                        strike kick bite
                            crush
—how do you resist?
    with a peaceful, wide
    field of golden oats?
    —or: another roaring
        regiment
            to confront
                the first?

—how? —so there remains
    green grass, a soft dark night
    a herder, a fire
        horses at pasture
            a rider riding home
                —so there remains a home
                to return home to

•

—es ārpus laika esmu.
Tu paver durvis, stikli čirkstot
saņem tavas basās pēdas,
tev plakstos triecas vējš, tu atver saujas,
un sēnalas un pelni dejo
vītnē bezgalīgā, sausā straumē
džinkstot tev caur pirkstiem
dzelzu meitas stingie mati
sitas, dzirkstis šķilot.
    —Mēs ārpus laika esam,
    ne aiziešanai esam sliekšņi,
    ne pārnākšanai esam.
    Es skatos nebūtībai tieši acīs
    un redzu savu dvīni.

"I exist outside of time"

I exist outside of time.
You open the door, and beneath your bare feet
crunches glass, wind rushes
into your eyes. You open your hands,
and husks and ashes dance
in an unending chain.

> —We exist outside of time.
> We are thresholds
> neither for leaving,
> nor returning.
> I look nonbeing in the eye,
> and I behold
> my twin.

(pirms notikuma)

—pelēka upe, bez trīsas,
bez vilnīša virsma,
nekustas straume,
laiva neelpo.
Viss stājies, i vējš, i mākoņi
vien vārdi grāmatā aizšķirtā.
Dievs pauzē,
Dievs ievelk elpu, pirms,
                    pirms—

(before)

A gray river, not a tremor:
the surface still,
the current motionless,
the boat not breathing.
All has stopped, wind, clouds,
only the words in an unopened book exist.
God has paused,
God takes a breath, before,
                    before—

Otrādi

—un pēkšņi tu jūti, ka
zemes lode, apsviedusies otrādi,
tricinās trīces grūdienos,
un tajā atveras plaisas,
un tu krīti
    taisni ar galvu
    zemes dziļumos iekšā,
    bet virs kājām tev
    plīvinās izplatījums,
    un vienā apžilbinātajā mirklī
    viss ap tevi saraustais,
    sastādītais
    sasprāgdams
        aizlido projām,
        —un tad, it kā šķilā ietēsts,
        tu rimsties
        un laid,
        lai pa tavu smadzeņu šķiedrām
        jaunu pasauļu sākumi staigā,
        un tavās ausīs saklaigājas
        vēl nedzirdētu valodu
        bērnudārzi,
        un pār taviem locekļiem
        tecētāji kalni
        un gulētājas upes,
        noskūti lauki
        un aizmežotas pilsētas
        stumdās
            šurpu un turpu,
            bet ap tavām debesīs
            atstieptām pēdām
            tālumi raustās.

Upside Down

And you suddenly feel
the earth has flung itself upside down,
shudders as if from a quake,
cracks open,
and you plunge
        headlong
        into its depths,
        above your feet
        flutters space,
        and in one dazzling instant
        all you have gathered,
        planted,
        explodes
            and vanishes;
            —and then, as if wedged in wood
            you grow calm,
            and let
            the beginnings of new worlds
            roam the filaments of your brain,
            let kindergartens
            of languages never heard
            call back and forth in your ears,
            and across your limbs
            you let hastening mountains
            and rivers asleep,
            shaved fields
            and cities overgrown by forests
            jostle.

•

Piens no visām krūzēm,
no visām pudelēm
        izliets un izdzerts,
uz visām sētām melno
apgāzti spaiņi.

    Tālīnās, tumsušās kūtīs
    saules tesmenis pamazām
                    pieriet un piebriest,
    agrīnā rītā
    no rožainiem pupiem
    gaisma kad strūklos,
    atkal piecelsies
    trauki un karotes,
    silta un balta valoda
            šļupstēs.

"When milk from every pitcher"

When milk from every pitcher,
from every bottle
            has been poured and drunk,
on each fence post at dusk
dims an upturned pail.

            In dark, faraway barns
            slowly an udder of sun
                        fills and swells;
            at daybreak,
            when from rosy teats light
            will stream,
            the sound of dishes and spoons will rise again,
            and the murmur
                        of morning's warm language.

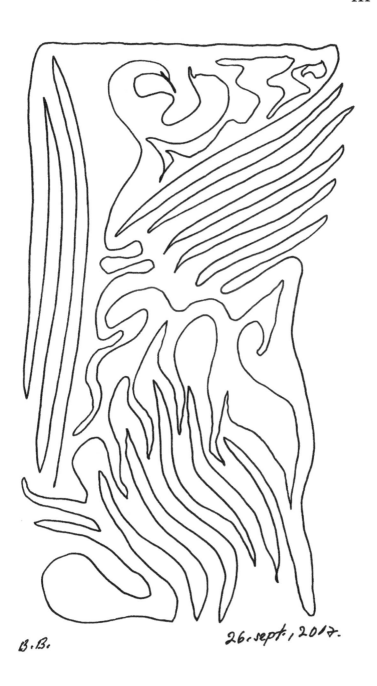

B. B.

26. sept, 2017.

●

—un šī ir karsta vasara;
tu atver mežu līdz galam,
un es ieeju skuju biršanā
                karstumā,
un es ieeju zvēru elsās
                karstumā
        ūdeni meklējot,
un tu atver ceļu līdz galam,
un akmeņi viļājas, cilājas
                sprēgājot
                karstumā,
un tu atveri debesis līdz galam,
un nokrīt mēness kā pārplīsdams ābols,
                kā dzeltena plūme, un
apšļakstās mežs un celš,
un mēs, karstumā kūstot,
        lipīgām mutēm un rokām.

"And this summer is hot"

And this summer is hot;
you open the forest all the way,
and I enter the pine needles falling
                            in the heat,
and I enter the panting of beasts
                            searching for water
                            in the heat,
and you open the road all the way,
and the stones roll and lift,
                    splintering
                    in the heat,
and you open the heavens all the way,
and the moon falls like a bursting apple,
                    like a yellow plum, and
splashes the forest and road,
and we, our mouths and hands sticky, melt
                            in the heat.

Mīlestība

Bij tikai pirkstu saskaršanās
un mirklis gaismas
                    uzzibsnīšanās,
ieņemšana bij bezvainīga.
Bet piedzima bērns,
un tad, kad to savām asinīm
                    baroju,
no savas dvēseles dzirdināju,
auklēju un apmātās spēkā
ļāvu, lai aug,
sākās mana vaina un
                    grēks.

Ik diena, ik nakts nu
izbaiļu drebināta—
vai arī šo, gaišo, stipro
                    un labo,
pienaglos krustā?

Love

It was only a touching of fingertips
and a moment's flash
                    of light,
an immaculate conception.
But a child was born,
and then, when I fed it
                    with my blood,
had it drink from my soul,
cradled it, and with the strength of the possessed
let it grow,
began my transgression and
                              sin.

Each day, each night now
is shaken by fear—
will this one too, filled with light, strong
                                        and good,
be nailed to the cross?

Pa dzirkstīm kad brists

Pa dzirkstīm kad brists,
pēdas mācos kā pelnus izkaisīt
                              vējos,
lai nejauš sekotājs,
apsvilušos matus arvien īsākus
                              apgriežu,
gruzduma sprogas
lai neredz vērotājs.

Bet šorīt ietves ir ledus
spoguļi,
un mani sasalušie pirksti
grieznes nenotur,
un visās vīlēs smaržo dūmi.

—Kādi soļi švīkst.
Es atskatos—

        kāds smags un tumšs
        man seko,
        smilšu maiss kuļājas plecos,
        —ai! pirms mani apber,
        man jāsadeg!

When I Have Walked Through Sparks

When I have walked through sparks,
to fool the follower
I cast my footprints into the wind
                              like ashes,
my singed hair I cut
                    ever shorter,
so no eye will see.

    But the sidewalks this morning are mirrors
    of ice,
    my numb fingers let fall
    the scissors,
    and from every seam seeps the odor of smoke.

        The scrape of footsteps.
        I look back—

           A figure heavy and dark
           is following me,
           across the shoulder a swaying sack of sand;
           —before it is strewn,
                I must burn up.

•

No jumtu platmalēm, no palodu
                       plakstieniem
klusa un mīksta vakara valoda
lēnītēm pakš,
skaņa uz skaņas, zīme aiz
               zīmes—
slepenā ūdeņu grāmata
            rakstās.

Piesmeļu plaukstu, iemērcu matus—
tu maigām lūpām
pieskaries man,
un visu nakti
debesu zintis
manā augumā
          lasi.

"Like rain from the brim of a roof"

Like rain from the brim of a roof,
from a lintel's
           eyelid,
slowly drop
evening's quiet words,
sound upon sound, sign behind
                          sign:
being written
      is the secret book of waters.

      I scoop up a handful, I immerse my hair—
      you touch me softly
      with your lips,
      and all night long
                    read
      from my body
      the wisdom of the sky.

(no Mīlētāju dziesmām)

I

neredzami
tavās ausīs
tie ienāk
vārdi
tavu roku piepešās
kustības
atsedz
melodiju

II

tik apvaldītam
tik uzmanīgam
būt
pat mats uz grīdas
saules skarts
dzirksteļo

III

—no manas rokas tavā rokā
sarkans āboliņš
pirksti: trīsu desmitnieks

(from Lovers' Songs)

I

they enter your ears
invisibly,
    the words

        your hand's sudden
                movement
            reveals
        the melody

II

to be
so contained
so careful
    even a hair on the floor
      touched by sunlight
        sparkles

III

—from my hand into yours
    red clover, ten fingers
      trembling

●

Haiku mirkļi,
sīkās pastmarkas,
pasaules apceļotājas.

*

Tavs krekls, lidlauks,
kur nosēžas mana roka,
mājās pārnākdama.

"Haiku moments"

Haiku moments:
tiny postage stamps,
world travelers.

*

Your shirt, an airfield
on which my hand sets down,
returning home.

•

—Tavs klusums—krāsas:
　　pelēka migla pār ostu,
　　košsarkana kuģa pulss,
　　bojas liesmainā acs,
　　　krastā namu ķekars
　　　　　　tumšzils,
　　　　briest apvārsnī plūme
　　　　　　mēļa,
　　　arvien mēļāka,
　　　gatavāka
　　　pārsprāgst,
　　šļācas
　zibens sula
　　tumšzelta
　　　žilbinoša
(Tu man vēstuli raksti)

"Your silence—colors"

Your silence—colors:
      gray mist above the harbor,
      a red ship's pulse,
      the fiery eye of a buoy,
        on the shore, a cluster of buildings
                        in indigo;
        on the horizon a plum,
                purple,
           darkens,
          ripens,
        bursts:
           lightning's liquor gushes
          dark gold,
             dazzling

       (you are writing a letter to me)

•

—jau izraku vietu jūrai
　　starp mums,
　　gaidīju debesis atveŗamies,
　　gaidīju milzīgus plūdus, kam
　　piepildīt izrakto vietu
　　ar ūdeņiem, dzelmēm,
　　viļņiem
　　briesmīgiem.

　　Tas viss notika.

　　　　Un mēs? —Katrs no sava krasta
　　　　pār ūdeņiem gājām,
　　　　vidū jūras
　　　　satikāmies.

"In the vastness between us"

In the vastness between us,
    I hollowed a place
    for a sea.
        I waited for the heavens to open,
        I waited for a wondrous flood
        to fill the hollow
        with waters, deeps,
        terrible
        waves.

    It all came to pass.

        And we? —You and I, from our separate shores,
        walked across the waters to meet
                in mid-sea.

•

—mīlestības mēļu mēles:
asiņainā mēle
mēle ērkšķainā
mēle lauks pilns ziedos
        magoņu un āboliņa sārtna
noslēptā mēle aizslēgtā mute
(aizdurvē mēmais raustās mokās)
udenskrituma mēle
uguņu mēle
mēle no akmens
akmeņu šļūdoņa mēle
saldā medusmēle un
sālījumu lāsodama mēle
uz mēles degošais krūms
mēle buras un vējš (un
        ceļojums sākas)
mēles urbums līdz dzīlei
(vaļā robežas viss)
miera mēle paraksti izlīgumam
(oāze zila dzirkstīga ūdenskrūze
        tuksnesis—ārpus)
        mēle kas pasauli piedzied

"—the tongues and tongues of love"

—the tongues and tongues of love:
the wounded tongue
a thorny tongue
the tongue a field of wildflowers,
                          the redness of poppies and clover
the hidden tongue, a locked mouth
(behind the door a mute in torment)
a waterfall tongue
a tongue of fires
a tongue of stone
the tongue of falling rocks
a sweet honey-tongue and
the salt tongue
on a tongue the burning bush
a tongue, a sail, and wind (and
                          the journey begins)
the tongue that bores down to the core
(borders open, and worlds)
the tongue of peace, signatures for reconciliation
                  (a blue oasis, a pitcher of sparkling water)
a tongue that fills the world with song

IV

15. jūnijs 2017

Pastaigas

I

—uz lietussarga lietus lāšu ritmi
vienmērīgie,
minimālisms, Filips Glāss spēlē
klavieres,
zālē, kokos un krūmos zaļums
vācu ekspresionistu un fovistu
maksimālais,
bet Filips Glāss turpina spēlēt,
vienmērīgos ritmos turpina līt,
es domāju par pulksteņa tikšķiem,
sirds pukstiem un par biezā zaļā zālē
noslēpušamies nevienmērīgām bailēm.

Walking

I

Against the umbrella, the rhythm of even
                                        raindrops:
minimalism—Philip Glass playing
                        the piano;
in the greenness of grass, trees, bushes,
fauvist and German expressionist
                        maximalism,
but Philip Glass continues to play,
the raindrops, to rain evenly—
I think about the ticking of clocks,
heartbeats, and fears in thick green grass, hidden
and uneven.

●

—apskapstējusi siena,
grumbas un rievas,
nekas te nav līdzens,
nekā te gludeni skaista.
Mani saista šis raupjums,
juceklis krāsu un
sen sabirzušu roku kustības
paliekamās.

"—a rough wall"

—a rough wall,
ridged and pitted;
there is nothing smooth here,
there is nothing beautiful.
I am drawn
to this roughness,
this confusion of colors,
these crumbling traces
of a hand's long-ago
movement.

•

—manu redzesloku
 šķērso puteklis, pārlido
 rudens lapa, sniegpārsla
    pārdejo,
  ieaug koks, iestatās nams,
  manā redzeslokā ievirzās
      cilvēks.
  Man vesela pasaule tuvu.

"—across my field of vision"

—across my field of vision
 drifts a speck of dust, flies
  an autumn leaf, a snowflake
            dances,
    a tree, a house take root;
      into my field of vision steps
                a person.
  —Before me, an entire world.

Ņujorkas Klosteŗos

No sienas pusspraucies
vizlā ielipis
akmens eņģelītis,
pret pasauli nobrāzis seju,
bez acīm, bez vaibstiem
akmens smagumā
spārnu vieglumu vēstī.

At the Cloisters, New York

As if pulled halfway out of the wall,
immobile in limestone,
a small stone angel:
face scraped against the world,
with no eyes, without features,
in his stone heaviness, he heralds
the lightness of wings.

(Pa vagona logu)

*

Baznīctorņi,
   ceļamkrānu smailes,
      vēl augstāk mākoņi,
         caur tiem saulstaru strēles—
      vertikāļu sasaukšanās.
        Dieva darbs.

*

Augsta, gaismu izstarojoša piere—
   starp apvāršņa svītru un
         mākoņu grēdām
           debess atvērums.

*

Dievs, akmeņu akmens,
spārnu spārni,
tumšā un gaišā gaisma.

(through the window of a train)

*

Steeples of churches,
    spires of cranes,
        even higher, clouds
               pierced by streaks of sun—
               verticals, calling one to another.
            God's work.

*

Between the stripe of the horizon and
    the piled-up clouds,
        like a steep, radiant brow
               an intimation
                   of the heavens.

*

God—stone of stone,
a feeling of wings,
the dark light, and the luminous one.

Drupas Grieķijā

Man tuvojoties,
tūkstošgadu nobrucinātais mūris
žigli aizzogas mežrožu mudžeklī.
Lupstāji šļupst,
augstajos zaros
klakšķina putni,
        —tai takā tā kā
        it nekā—
klinšu sarkanās mēles
atbalsīs mēdās—
                nekā,
                  nekā—
                Smalkas drumslas vizuļo acīs.
                Dienvidus sirsina.
                Saule plēš plecus.
                    Nokrītu ceļos:

                te ir tā vieta,
                kur izcirtās
                pirmais tēls,
                un dievi žūžoja ausīs

Ruins in Greece

As I near,
the ancient stone wall
steals into a tangle of wild roses.
The lovage whispers,
birds in high branches cry,
                    not here,
                        not here—

the cliffs' red tongues
echo,
      not here,
          not here—

                Glint of delicate shards.
                From the south, a chirring sound.
                The sun scorching my shoulders.
                    I fall to my knees:

                This is the place
                where out of stone the first
                image emerged,
                and gods
                hummed in your ear.

V

B.B.   19. jūlijs, 2022

Ai, kā griezušies vēji

I

Ai, kā griezušies vēji, ai,
kā sviedušies sniegi, ai,
kā nu aizmidzināti visi ceļi,
visas ielas, logi pa pusei,
durvis pa sprīdim vairs
laužas pret sala elkoņiem asiem,
bet skurstenis ar dūmu vīkšķi
aizsedz aci,
saka—vēl silta,
vēl mana acs silta,
vēl mājas sirds
pukst.

II

Tām dienām šļūdoņa plūdums.
Slīd gausi, un tomēr koki
                              un krūmi brakšķ,
jaunu akmeņu smagums
ieglaužas ledos un sniegos.

    Bet tie putni,
    kas saules medībās
                  pāri lido,
    jau zina,
    ka aiz jūklainām jūdzēm
    gaida jūra
    un lielā pārvēršanās.

Oh, How the Winds Have Turned

I

Oh, how the winds have turned, oh,
how snows have been thrown about, oh,
how all the roads have fallen asleep,
all the streets, windows halfway;
doors no longer resist
the sharp elbows of winter,
but the chimney covers
its eye
with a wisp of smoke
and says, it is still warm—
my eye is still warm,
the heart of the house
is still beating.

II

The days move slowly—slow
as glaciers, yet trees and bushes
                                    rustle,
into the ice and snow
settles the weight of new rocks.

        But the birds
        flying over,
                    chasing the sun,
        know that beyond the muddled miles
        waits the sea
        and the great transformation.

Padoms gleznotājam

Ar lietu iekaŗos
jumtu un koku ķekaros,
ar vēju, ar sauli iekūstu ielās,

tu brīnies un zūdies,
ka manu seju nevari
audeklā tvert,

—glezno šīs kustības ņirbu,
mijas mirkli,
tumsas lēcienu gaismā
un atlocīšanos atpakaļ.

Advice to a Painter

Together with rain, I cling to clusters
of leaves, with wind and sun,
I melt into the streets—

you marvel and complain
you cannot capture my face
on canvas:

> —paint the iridescence of movement,
> instant of transformation,
> the leap of darkness into light,
> and the inching back.

•

—saule
    saule rej
        suns zeltainu zīžainu spīdīgu
                spalvu
        saule
      suns kas piesiets
        savam kalnā kāpienam
        savai lejupslīdei
        jūŗā
           nogrimšanai

—klusuma jūŗa
mirguļo mēness
    ir mēms
      pat neelpo—

"—the sun"

—the sun
      the sun barking:
          a dog, its coat golden, silken,
                    shining

           the sun
          a dog tethered
                to climbing its mountain
                the slide downward
                into the sea
                    the sinking

—a sea of silence
the glimmering moon
          mute
             not even breathing

Skrējiens naktī

Nomazgājusies mēnesnīca,
bērnības spožumā zvaigznes,
augsto mežu melnās spuras,
pļavas ledainā rasa dzen skrieties—
pēdas pus lidojot—
vai esmu zaķis, savu sirdspukstu tramdīts?
—vieglums bez gala—
vai naktsputns tumsas gudrību spārnu galos?

Running in the Night

Moonlight rinsed clean,
stars as bright as in childhood,
the forest's black, bristly treetops,
the icy dew in the meadow—all
compel me to run—
my feet half flying:
am I a hare driven by a pounding heart
—lightness without end—
or a nightbird,
in its wingtips the wisdom of night?

•

Uzzīmēta
  izkrāsota
    izgriezta
      ielīmēta
        nedzīva saule
        nedzīvās debesīs.
        Tu mani taujā, kā
        šodien jūtos.
        "Spoguļus vairos."

"The sun, lifeless"

The sun, lifeless,
   drawn
      painted
         cut out
            pasted into
            a lifeless sky.
                  You ask me how
                  I feel today.
                  "I turn away from mirrors."

(bīstamā vietā)

—neuzticos zemei,
neuzticos sev,
te lodenas, mānīgi glaudenas
                      virsmas,
melnstikla duravas, logi,
zemi te slieksņi
no vienas saules
uz otru.

(in a dangerous place)

—I do not trust the earth,
I do not trust myself:
the surfaces here are smooth,
                    deceptively soothing,
the doors and windows black glass,
the doorsills low
that lead from this sun
into the next.

Atnākušais

Kad atkal iznākam ielā,
to atrodam nosirmojušu.
Bijīgi iet, caur baltiem krūmiem
izlaist pirkstus
un sajust
atnākušā ledus laikmeta
pirmās šķiedras.

Iztrūcinātos logos
kā slēpšanās? kā padošanās zīmes?
blāvas ledus puķes.
Stiklos karājas sejas.

Es ievēroju—
nami kā dinozauri
sākuši šķiebties
ne atmodai,
        miegam,
                bet es nerunāju,

manu pēdu ļoganais raksts
jau ir skaidrāks
par manas mutes stinstošo čukstu.

Manas lūpas
divas ledus šķilas
nokrīt un saplīst,
atbalss vientuļā,
prātā jukusī, sieviete
aizskrien.

Arrival

When we come out on the street again,
we find it covered in frost.
We run our fingers across
the white bushes
and touch, with reverence,
the first filaments
of the newly arrived
ice age.

> In the disturbed windows, wan
> ice flowers—signs of hiding? of surrender?
> Behind the glass, haggard faces.

>> Buildings,
>> like the dinosaurs,
>> have begun to lean—
>> as if for sleep,
>>> but I keep silent,

>> the prints of my unsteady steps
>> clearer
>> than a numb whisper.

>> My lips,
>> two slivers of ice,
>> fall and shatter,
>> and like a lone, crazed woman,
>> the echo
>> flees.

Laimes meklētājs

Tu gaidi ar dzirkstelēm pirkstos,
tu ausies sirds pukstos sienās,
tu sadzirdi elsas zemes slāņos,
tu bīsties zemes lodes pāršķelšanās,
tu bīsties savu senču kaulu piecelšanās,
jo tu pirmais pacēli lāpstu,
un tavās raktuvēs
ugunsgrēks plosās.

The Fortune Seeker

You wait—your fingertips like sparks,
you listen, for heartbeats in walls,
you hear sobbing through the layers of earth,
you fear the earth's splitting apart,
you fear the bones of your ancestors rising—
for you were the first
to pick up a spade, and in your mines
a wildfire rages.

Par lapsu

Laime ir putns,
kas tevi no biezokņa biezoknī trenkā,

laime ir ganāmpulks,
ko apsargā gans, rīkste un suns,

laime ir ceļš,
kura zīmēs tu neapstājies,

laime ir cilpa,
kurā tavs spurainais kakls neaizķeras,

laime? —lamatas,
kas norauj tavu skaisto, kuplo asti,

tavās dzeltenās acīs laime sāp,
                    lapsa.

About the Fox

Happiness is the bird you chase
thicket to thicket,

happiness is a herd
guarded by herder, switch, and dog,

happiness is the road
whose signs you don't heed,

happiness is a noose
the fur on your neck doesn't catch in,

happiness? —a snare
that tears off your bushy, beautiful tail;

your golden eyes, fox, sting
                    from happiness.

•

Viņa izgāja laukā,
pacēla galvu, skatījās
augšup,
skatījās ilgi:
nelīs vai līs?
Debesis arī šoreiz
nenodeva sevi,
ne savu kārtību,
ne sajukumu.

"She went outside"

She went outside,
raised her head,
        looked up,
     looked a long time:
        would there be rain?

Even this time, the sky revealed
neither its order,
nor its confusion.

●

Brūns izkaltis vakars
nakts vējam ziedojamās
ziedu lapas
skaita—

rīt dzirksteļojot
saule lēkās
stublājos bez galvām,

maigi un bez žēlām
tuksnesis dzeltēnu tīklu
pārvilks pār dārzu.

"A brown, parched evening"

A brown, parched evening
is counting
the petals to be offered
to the night wind—

       tomorrow a sparkling
       sun will skip
       through headless stalks,

       and gently, without regret,
       the desert will pull a yellow net
       across the garden.

•

Atkala, manā dārzā
koki, manā dārzā
krusti, ik krustā
spožām naglām
pienaglots eņģelis.

"An ice storm"

An ice storm—in my garden
trees, in my garden
crosses, on each cross,
nailed with bright
nails, an angel.

●

Salam ilkņi, salam kūpoša elpa,
un salam sirds,
kas manu sirdi
                    prasa.
Tas meklē, tas atrod,
tas savos dziļumos
                    noslēpj.
Es aizeju tālāk
kalsnāka, saltāka,
                    bālāka,
dzi, kā dzindzina
jau manos kaulos
                    ledi,
kā lāstekas no matiem
nokarājas, sīvi skanot,
un birst no pašas saujām
                    sniegi,
cisas būs nu kupenā.

"Coldness"

Coldness with tusks, with steaming breath,
and a heart
that demands
          mine.
It searches, finds it,
hides it deep
          within.
I walk on
gaunt, colder,
          paler—
ice already jangles
in my bones,
with a bitter sound
icicles hang from my hair,
and snow spills
          out of my hands;
—my bed will now
be snow.

·

Klusām ienācis, kāds dziļi elpo,
un karsta tam dvaša.
Manas puķes izslejas,
no lapām nopurinot
           ziemu,
viegli nodrebot,
tuvojas logam.
    Silts svīdums, garaiņu apmulsums
    sakāpj to stāvos, sāk blāvot ziedi,
    krāsām arvienu tumšākām satekot,
                    sarecot—
    bišu gaidas.

Un tad es sadzirdu
klusus vaidus, nopūtas, elsas,
—caur sniega puteņu miglu
skatās kāds cietām un bālām acīm,
ik solī tuvojotos, lāsteku šķinda,

        tas izpleš savu cimdoto sauju
        un tūkstoti mirušu bišu
                sviež stiklos—
     dzinn, dzinn—kā smalki ledi
            krīt
                un
                  krīt.

(the awaiting of bees)

Having entered unheard,
someone is breathing softly,
the breath warm.
My flowers straighten,
shake winter
off their leaves,
and lightly trembling, near the window.
A warm vapor, a giddiness
swells the stems, blossoms begin to glow,
colors blend, darken,
clot—
the awaiting of bees.

And then I hear
quiet moans, sighs, sobbing;
—through a blizzard's mist
someone is looking with hard, pale eyes,
and with each approaching step,
I hear the clinking of icicles:

he opens his mittened hand, and flings
against the glass
thousands of dead bees—
like splinters of ice,
they fall
and
fall.

(Agrā pavasarī)

Spēji
  sagriezās vēji,
    gaisos dūcīši asi,
      sniegpārslu zibā
        pirmo ziedlapu
          dvēselītes.

(in early spring)

Abruptly
    the wind shifts:
        in the air, small sharp knives,
            and amid a streak of snowflakes
          the tiny souls
              of the earliest petals.

Vējdziesmas

I

—saskrējāmies es un vējš
atsitāmies viens otrā
        es un vējš
    ne uzauga puni
    ne zilumu ēnas
    ne skrambas uz ādas
        tik viegli
        glaudāmies
        vijāmies tīteniski
        saaudāmies
            es un vējš—

Windsongs

I

—we ran into each other, the wind and I,
we collided,
       the wind and I,
    no bruises appeared
    no blue shadows
    no scraped skin—
        we brushed
        so lightly
        we intertwined,
               the wind and I

II
—tagad
man liekas
    vējš
    kaut kāds
    jebkurš
    jebkurā brīdī
        vējš
        varētu piepeši
        pacelties spārnos
        plašu piepeši
            izpūst elpu
            aizpūst mani
            projām
            no zemes vaiga
            kā pūku
            mākonīti
            sīku
            kukainīti
        kaut kad
        jebkurā dienā
        stundā
    tas var notikt
eņģeļvējš
eņģeļvējš
un es—

II

—now
I imagine
a wind
of any kind
at any moment
a wind
might sudddenly
take wing,
with a puff
blow me off
the face of the earth
like down
a light cloud
a tiny
insect
it might happen
any day
any hour—
angel wind
angel wind
and I

•

Bieza, bieza migla starp kokiem.
Visaugstākās egles galotne jau
                          izkususi,
zem zariem zaļa ūdens acs.
Tā debess, kas atnes, kas aiznes,
šodien staigā caur dārziem,
mīkstiem pelēkiem pirkstiem
appaijā stumbrus, kailos
vārīgos zarus, čabinās
kritušās lapās, pie ziemcietēm saknēm
sniedzas ar garu ūdens roku.
Putni kustas pilošiem spārniem.
Uz sētas mēlenes bārkstis.

Mana māja iekārta
miglas šūpulī, debesīs,
kas atnes, kas aiznes.

"Between the trees"

Between the trees, a dense mist.
The tip of the tallest spruce already
                              dissolved,
beneath the branches, a green eye of water.
The sky that brings, that takes away,
is walking through gardens today—
soft, gray fingers stroke the trunks, the fragile
bare boughs; it rustles through fallen leaves,
to overwintering roots
extends a long water-arm.
Birds move with dripping wings.
Along a fence,
like the fringe of an indigo shawl,
a row of waterdrops.

My dwelling is hung
in a cradle of mist—
in the sky that brings, that takes away.

Novembris I

Dārzos zviln deguma smaka
zilganās drānās
un lapu nāves vietu sargā
gruzdošiem pirkstiem,

—spējš
pelnos iesitas
nemiera puksts,

—sarkana mēle
laizās ar vēju,
gaŗi mati dzirksteļu gredzenos
pinas,

vasaras veļi dejo
kvēlošām sejām,

gailošām drānām
debessbraukšanai
paceļas koks.

November

In the gardens,
the odor of burning sprawls
like a blue garment
on the ground,
and smoldering fingers guard
the leaves'
place of death;

      —a sudden restlessness
      pulses
      through the ash

      —a red tongue
      licks at the wind, sparks swirl
      like long strands of hair,

            and faces burning,
            the Shades of summer dance—

            robed in a glowing cloak,
            a tree
            ascends into the heavens.

Tam, kurš gribēja projām

—un, pacēlis apvāršņa sānu uz augšu,
viņš atrada atkal citu—
kāpostu lapas,
sīpolu mizas,
liepu lūki
plēšami, mizojami, lobāmi—
zemi bez malas—
bet zvaigžņu asums
tam kutināja pēdas un plecus,
vilka tam plakstos ik nakti—
      un, klusām noslēpies biezoknī,
      viņš kļuva putnu pētnieks,
      sarkana akmens šķēpeli
      vilkdams uz klints,
      zīmēja spārnus,
            spārnus—
      un pamazām izdila
      plāns un viegls kā putns,
      kā taurenis, kā vissīkākā kode,
      kā puteklis no zvaigznes.

The One Who Wanted to Get Away

He tipped up the horizon,
and beneath it found an older world—
with cabbage,
onions,
the bark of lindens,
to be cut, peeled, plaited—
a world without end;
    but the sharpness
    of stars
    tickled his shoulders and soles,
    tugged each night at his eyelids—
and silent, hidden in thickets,
        he became a student of birds:
        drawing on cliffs,
        with a red sliver of stone, wings,
                wings—
        and slowly he grew
        thin and light as a bird,
        as a butterfly, the tiniest moth,
        as a speck of dust
        from a star.

Notes

"—and then I wanted to taste the river" Oriole: In Latvian folk belief, in times of drought the oriole calls for rain.

(in a dangerous place) The "next sun": In Latvian folklore, the afterworld is depicted as a place beyond the sun, the "other sun," whereas life on earth is beneath "this sun."

The One Who Wanted to Get Away Linden bark: The allusion is to the peeled and woven bark of linden trees used for making bast shoes, worn in the past by the Latvian peasantry.

Sources of the Poems

The poems have been selected and arranged by the translator from the following publications. (Full publication credits appear on the copyright page.)

Ceļos (1969): "The evening has been folded"; "A drop of sun"; (before); "A brown, parched evening"; November

Buŗot (1976): At a Funeral; Upside Down; When I Have Walked Through Sparks; Ruins in Greece; Oh, How the Winds Have Turned; Running in the Night; Arrival; The Fortune Seeker; About the Fox; The One Who Wanted to Get Away

Griežos (1981): "—and then I wanted to taste the river"; "The earth"; Ancestral Mother; "I am the skin of a drum"; Separated; Before a Painting; Weeping; "through the heavy stone wall"; "I exist outside of time"; "When milk from every pitcher"; "And this summer is hot"; Love; "Like rain from the brim of a roof"; Advice to a Painter; "Coldness"; (the awaiting of bees); "Between the trees"

Atgriežos (1991): Desert

Citviet (2011): (from a dream diary); "As if this day were unending"; "I turn"; (the mute ones); "—when heavy horses"; (from Lovers' Songs); "Haiku moments"; "Your silence—colors"; "In the vastness between us"; "the tongues and tongues of love"; Walking; "—a rough wall"; "—across my field of vision"; At the Cloisters, New York; (through the window of a train); "—the sun"; "the sun, lifeless"; (in a dangerous place); "She went outside"; "An ice storm"; (in early spring)

Latvju teksti (November 5, 2014): "today"; Windsongs

Acknowledgments

Grateful acknowledgment is made to the editors of the following journals and anthology:

Arts & Letters: Desert; (the mute ones); "As if this day were unending"

Circumference: (from a dream diary)

Denver Quarterly: "—and then I wanted to taste the river"; Upside Down; "the tongues and tongues of love"; "She went outside"

Epiphany: "I exist outside of time"; "through the heavy stone wall"; "In the vastness between us"

In Transit: Poems of Travel, eds. Sarah Jackson and Tim Youngs (Birmingham, UK: The Emma Press): Walking

Jaunā gaita (The New Path): "—and then I wanted to taste the river"; Before a Painting; "And this summer is hot"

Kenyon Review: Separated; November

The Manhattan Review: Before a Painting; "A drop of sun"

The Massachusetts Review: (siege)

Spillway: "And this summer is hot"

A very warm thank-you to the author, Baiba Bičole, for the many enjoyable and invaluable conversations about her work and individual poems, and for the flexibility and freedom she has given me in the rendering of her poems into a different language.

To the editor and publisher, Roman Kostovski, whom it has been a pleasure to work with, gratitude for his care in guiding the book through production and beyond.

About the Author

Baiba Bičole, born in Latvia in 1931, left as a refugee during World War II, and since 1950 has lived in the United States. Though she has been a major Latvian poet since the 1970s, until Latvia regained its independence in 1991, she was known primarily in the West, as an exile poet, her work banned in Soviet-occupied Latvia. She is the author of six collections of poetry, and has received important Latvian literary awards, from the Zinaīda Lazda Foundation, the Raisters Foundation, and the World Federation of Free Latvians (PBLA). For many years she taught Latvian literature in Latvian American schools and was the editor of the Latvian newspaper *Laiks*.

This is her first poetry collection in English translation.

About the Translator

Bitite Vinklers is a translator of Latvian folklore and contemporary literature. Her translations have been published in numerous anthologies and journals, including *The Paris Review, Kenyon Review, The Massachusetts Review,* and *Two Lines.* Recent translation collections include Imants Ziedonis, *Each Day Catches Fire: Poems* (Red Dragonfly Press, 2015); Knuts Skujenieks, *Seed in Snow: Poems* (BOA Editions, 2016); and Aleksandrs Čaks, *Poems* (Riga, Latvia: Jumava Press, 2018). She lives and works as an editor in New York.

CPSIA information can be obtained
at www.ICGtesting.com
Printed in the USA
FSHW010816211021
85586FS